THAT'S LIFE!

Featuring the Wit and Wisdom of
Bernadette McCarver Snyder

LIGUORI
PUBLICATIONS

One Liguori Drive
Liguori, Missouri 63057-9999
(314) 464-2500

...dedication

With grateful appreciation, I dedicate this
book to Will Shaw, Ed Murray, and all the folks
associated with the radio apostolate
of the Missionary Oblates.

Several years ago they asked me to write and record
a series of short radio spots to be entitled "That's Life."
Since then, those spots have been aired regularly on
more than eighteen hundred stations across America.
From those spots, grew this book.

Thanks, Oblates.

ISBN 0-89243-408-2
Library of Congress Catalog Card Number: 91-62108

Cover design by Pam Hummelsheim

...introduction

Feeling frazzled, frustrated, fizzled out? Is your life like a sweater with little fuzzies all over it? When you try to make it better by pulling a loose thread, does the whole thing start to unravel? If you're a card-carrying member of the Great Unraveled, welcome to this semi-inspirational book of thoughts for the threadbare.

It was written for anyone who's down in the dumps or out in the suburbs. It admits that you have to take out a lot of trash before you find a rainbow in a plain brown wrapper. It doesn't pretend to offer psychological solutions for everyday glitches or theological revelations to save you from daily rumbles or rambles. It simply suggests that when you're down and out, you REFUSE to mope and pout. Why? Because frowns give you wrinkles. Smiles give you laugh lines — and then people begin to wonder what you've been up to!

So make someone wonder. Wonder yourself. Help yourself to a grin or a giggle, or maybe just a snort or a snicker. Go on! Try it. That's life!

...contents

That's Life!...around the house

That's Life!...around the town

That's Life!...with holiday seasonings

THAT'S LIFE!

...in the family

...not NOW!

"They just won't leave me alone!" How often you hear those words in a family. Mom says, "Did you finish your homework?" Tommy says, "Why can't you leave me alone?" Dad says, "Better hurry, you'll be late." Sue shouts, "I know the time! Leave me alone!" But that's the wonderful thing about being part of a family. They just won't leave you — alone! That's life.

...trickle, trickle, trickle

The trickle-down theory is finally taking effect at my house.

Water's trickling down the bathroom wall — SOMEONE sprayed it with the showerhead.

Milk's trickling down the leg of the kitchen table — SOMEONE bumped someone's elbow.

The budget's trickling down to zero...well, you get the picture.

We have lots of trickles in our family BUT we have lots of tickles too — and that's life!

...going all out

There are lots of family INS and OUTS. I can never get my kid IN the tub — but once he's in there, I can't get him out! I can never get my husband OUT of the house to go to a party — but once he's there, I can't get him IN the car to come home. But they're both MY GUYS, so — even when I'm all-in or outdone — I know I'll never pitch 'em OUT or trade 'em IN. That's life!

...trash or treasure?

Great-aunt Ermatrude said, "Aah, he has his father's eyes." Great-aunt Sue said, "and his mother's smile." And the kid said, "Yeah, and he's got his brother's pants."

Children hate hand-me-downs. It's only when we get older that we finally appreciate the hand-me-down photos in the family album, Grandma's antique teapot, and Grandpa's antique jokes. Don't wait till tomorrow to enjoy today's treasures. That's life!

...complain, complain

"Turn down that radio." "Shut that door." "Did you forget to put the trash out AGAIN?"

It's so EASY to criticize and accuse the family. Why is it so hard to remember to praise and applaud — to compliment little accomplishments and to LOOK for good qualities and successes instead of failures? Love disciplines — but also appreciates. That's life.

...the rocky road

Some people have family jewels; we have family rocks. There's the rock from a grammar-school field trip...the rock found on the beach during a summer vacation...the rock music that's broadcast from my son's bedroom to the whole neighborhood...and the rocking chair that's lasted through three generations.

We may not have valuable jewels, but we DO have valuable memories. That's life.

...this is NOT a recording

"Mommy, come quick!" "Daddy, look at this!"

Children are always calling on parents. Enjoy it while they're little. When they reach college age, the kids start calling COLLECT! Well, that's why it's so nice to be part of a family. There's always someone to call — who you need to chat, to share, or to ask for help. That's life.

...a magic moment!

When my husband and I were invited to a fancy party, I told him I was going to shop for a new dress that would make me look skinny but curvy, sophisticated, stylish, and ten years younger. He said, "I don't think that discount store where you shop has a MAGIC department!" Oh, well, it doesn't matter so much what you look like on the outside anyway...the real magic always comes from inside. That's life!

...a sicken-ing story

My car has a runny nose; its radiator sprung a leak!

My refrigerator has a cough: its motor has started wheezing!

My sink has that terrible, stuffed-up feeling; its garbage disposal is clogged again!

But the good news is that in the midst of all these terrible flu symptoms, the whole family feels just fine! So I'll just take two cookies and call a repair shop in the morning. That's life!

...the second time around

Our house is full of charming but slightly used furniture found at garage sales, so when we inherited a second-hand dog from a friend, my son told everyone we'd gotten a "used" dog. Oh, well, new things are nice but — like new friends — you have to be so careful with them. Bargain treasures — like old friends — have already been broken in, so they're comfortable to live with. That's life.

...what a bargain

If there's a grouch in your house, you might like to hear about Mr. Grumpy. One day his wife mentioned a neighbor who was so nice and always smiling. Mr. Grumpy said, "What's so special about that? Smiles are a dime a dozen." Then his wife looked at him sweetly and said, "Here's twenty cents, dear. Could I please have two dozen?" That's life!

...picking up the pieces

My family's going to pieces! Today on the family-room floor, I found pieces of a puzzle, pieces of a pizza, pieces of toys, clothes, newspapers, and pieces of things I didn't even recognize. I'd like to give them a PIECE of my mind! Oh, well, guess I'll just keep on TRYING to teach them that it's nice to be neat — and just keep on LOVIN' 'em to pieces!
That's life.

...time out!

We've GOT to get organized — a place
for everything and everything in its place,
a time to work, a time to eat, a time to
come and go, a time to check the
timetable! BUT children don't BELIEVE
life was made to be lived by the clock.
They want us to giggle and gaze at
rainbows, discover, delight, exult, enjoy.
Children teach us to take TIME OUT for
the really important things! And that's life.

...rent-a-family

A family's home is a nice place to visit, but who can live there? I mean…don't you sometimes wonder what it would be like to RENT the members of a family so you could return them at six o'clock? Don't wonder…living with all those people you call relatives may not be perfect, but it's a lot better than facing a cold, cruel world all by your lonesome. That's life.

THAT'S LIFE!

...with friends

...shimmering or simmering

Yesterday I visited a friend and admired her lovely copper teapot — all glistening and glowing in the sunshine, filled with a bouquet of fresh-cut flowers. Then I remembered my OWN copper teapot — stained, dented, used so much it'll never shine and glow again. But it DOES glow — with pleasure at the way it whistles while it works, boiling water so my friends and I can share fragrant cups of coffee and raaazzberry tea. Mmmmm... that's life!

...doubling and dividing

Feeling stressed? hurried, worried? All the magic gone out of your life? Well, just take two laughs and call a friend in the morning! Laughter is always the best medicine, and sharing your worries with a friend can help make trouble seem "all better." That's why they say friendship can double your joy and divide your grief. That's life.

...catching on

Kerchoo! Kerchoo! Did you ever catch a miserable cold? Sure, you did! Or did you? Some authorities say that colds are NOT catching. Some authorities also say that smiles and friendship and happiness are not catching. But were you ever in a crowd when you caught sight of a sweet little baby's face? And just then, the baby smiled at you! Did you smile back? Maybe smiles ARE catching — AND friendship AND happiness. That's life.

...I'm SO glad for you

I just ran into an old school friend who immediately told me all the wonderful things she had accomplished, achieved, and acquired since we last met.

Don't you just hate that?

Oh, well, even though WHAT you do in this life is important, it's more important to do the best with what you've got.

Whoever you are — wife, husband, mother, father, friend, brain surgeon, or Popsicle salesperson — be the BEST you can be. That's life!

...are you on the most-wanted list?

Look out! Here comes the enemy! Is it your mother or father, husband or wife, son or daughter, boss, or best friend? Sometimes the one you suddenly see as an enemy is actually the very someone who loves you lots or the someone who is trying to help you or help you help yourself. Look carefully at the people around you. Then look in the mirror. Is the enemy within? Sometimes, that's life.

...those saving ways

Why is it a woman will clean house and THROW OUT anything that's used-up, leftover, or worn out, but she'll SAVE empty boxes, ribbons, bows, and leftover wrapping paper? Even squeaky-clean houses have basements full of wrapping paper from birthdays, baby showers, and Christmas waaaay past. If yours is one of those houses, maybe you should throw out the paper but hold tight to the memories. That's life.

THAT'S LIFE!

...with children

...a sticky situation

The bad news is that kids have sticky fingers!

They leave sticky lollipop fingerprints on chairs, chewing gum globs on tables, and jelly doughnut dabs where you least expect to find them. Kids stick to everything — including your heart.

So that's the good news. Those sticky-fingered kids leave happy memories that will stick with you forever! That's life.

...turn on that light

My son is the light of my life! And I'm
sure you feel the same way about your
sons or daughters. Why not! From the day
they're old enough to reach a light switch,
they turn on and LEAVE ON every light
in the house! Well, who wants to live in
the dark? Electricity may be expensive,
but a house aglow with light and laughter
and love is well worth the price!
That's life.

...waste not

Do you think kids are wasteful? Actually, kids can make things go a long way. A kid can take one peanut-butter sandwich and make it go on his face, on his shirt, on the table, on the dog, and sometimes all the way across the room! It's parents who are wasteful. We waste time fussing about spills and spots when we should be taking time to enjoy those smiles and hugs and peanut-butter kisses. That's life.

...looking for rain

One day I stood looking at the sky with a child. Suddenly she said, "LOOK...in the clouds...it looks like a funny clown standing on his head...and there's an angel with big beautiful wings...and a puppy dog. Can't you see a lot in the clouds?" All I had seen was the lightning in the distance while I worried whether a storm was coming. Looking for trouble can make you miss a lot of joy. That's life.

...when the best is not enough

"I'll trade you my Mercedes for your Rolls Royce," said the one in the designer jeans. "Oh, no, I want the Porsche," replied the one with the high-fashion haircut. THIS was the conversation in the SANDBOX at the park as two kids traded toy cars! And I wondered if they would grow up to want "only the best" and then to look at it and say, "Is this all there is?" That's NOT life.

...M is for the many

Do you know what a sweater is? That's what a kid puts on when a mother gets cold. Do you know what a music lesson is? That's what a kid takes because "Mommy says so."

Do you know what sympathy and understanding and birthday parties and Christmas stockings and Easter baskets are? That's what kids get because a mother cares.

Mother's Day is celebrated once a year but LIVED every day by moms who know — THAT'S LIFE.

...abracadabra

Children are magic! If you don't believe it, just watch one DISAPPEAR when it's homework time!

See one produce an instant tummy ache when there's a chore to be done. Or pull a rabbit out of a hat when you've said absolutely NO MORE pets!

But children really ARE magic! Their giggles can turn NOs into maybes. Their wide-eyed wonder can open your eyes to new hope and joy and love. That's life.

...getting in touch

Aren't kids fun...aren't they adorable...aren't they great to be around — as long as they live ACROSS THE STREET? You wouldn't want them any closer than THAT would you? Sure you would! You've gotta get close to a kid to play games and share secrets and have fun together.

Sometimes the best way to get in touch with a child is to get in touch with the child inside yourself. That's life.

...giving the very best

Kids love presents — and you want them to have the best, don't you? Better than YOU had!

Some folks shop till they drop — to give their kids terrific toys, great clothes, bigger homes, and world-class vacations.

But you know the best gift you can give a child — OR a friend or relative?

The gift of your time. A listening ear, an understanding smile, time for a game or a story, time for a tear or a chuckle. A handshake, a hug, reassurance of your faith and hope in the future. That's life.

...atten-SHUN

Has your kid ever come home with a report card and told you that A is for awful, B is for bad, but F and D are for fine and dandy?

Oh, you have to pay close attention when you're dealing with someone as shrewd as a child.

But maybe that's all children really want — and need — some of your close attention.

If there's a child in your life, please pay attention. That's life.

...prints charming

Some families have flowered wallpaper.
We have FINGERPRINTED wallpaper.
You don't need the FBI to tell you that
lollipop fingerprints point to a preschooler
and airplane-glue fingerprints to a crafty
middle-grader. And those dirty
fingerprints on the ceiling must mean the
teenager's been jumping for joy! Oh, well,
flowers are nice, but fingerprints are a
touching reminder of the special people
who have passed this way — and left their
mark! That's life.

...taking your lumps

Why is it the kid who decorated the dog with barbecue sauce, hosed out the living room for you, and used your best towels to clean a muddy skateboard is the very same one who makes you homemade valentines, has the cutest toothless grin, and whispers "I love you" when you least expect it!

Yep, the same kid who gives you a pain in the neck gives you a lump in the throat. That's life.

THAT'S LIFE!

...in the neighborhood

...going, going, not quite gone

I think I'll have a garage sale! I just looked at my garage and it's so dirty I'll never get it clean — I better sell it. Then I'll have a YARD sale and sell that crab grass. And a fire sale and sell that greasy oven. And a...okay...I know! I know! I should scrub a little harder every day and things wouldn't get like this! Just like living...to KEEP it clean, you gotta work on it every day. And then you'll never feel like selling out! That's life.

...keeping up

Some people have everything — money, fame, power, prestige...hang-ups, breakdowns, fears, failures, and the heartbreak of a bad haircut. Maybe we shouldn't complain about not having EVERYTHING or not being able to keep up with the Frothingwells.

Maybe it's best to just have enough to get by — with a little bit left over to share. That's life.

...the befores and afters

Don't you just love those "before" and "after" pictures — where they take a lady and make her over with a wild new hairdo or take a room and redo it with splashy colors and exotic décor? You know what? Sometimes I like the looks of the BEFORE better than the after!

They say beauty is in the eye of the beholder — so don't be "beholden" to society. Dress and act and BE the way you know in your heart is right. That's life.

...another new wrinkle

I don't even know anything about the newest wrinkle in fashion, yet I always seem to be wearing wrinkles! The wrinkle godmother must come in the night and put wrinkles in my clothes, on my face, AND in my life.

Oh, well, smooth can be boring, so we might as well learn to iron out those daily wrinkles — with patience, hope, and a lot of STARCH in the upper lip. That's life.

...all the trimmings

Have you noticed how much modern life resembles a TACO? A lot of trimmings, very little meat, and all wrapped up in a shell that's so fragile it breaks when you bite into it? Maybe it's time to toss out some of those trimmings to make room for something with a little more substance...time to take a bigger bite of morality, responsibility, honesty, and compassion. That's life.

...getting it together

At the glamorous fashion show, the fashion coordinator kept telling us to "pull it all together!" "Just wear a special belt or scarf — that will PULL IT ALL TOGETHER." I tried a belt and looked like a flour sack tied in the middle. I tried a scarf and looked like Jesse James' mother. I think it takes more than a belt or a scarf — it takes work and faith and hope and joy to really "pull yourself together." That's life.

...bigger but not better

Sensational...stupendous...terrific...
tremendous. My car is better, my house is
bigger, my friends are more famous.

Everywhere you go today you hear brag,
brag, brag. But do you ever hear anyone
bragging about integrity, faithfulness, high
morals, kindness, and just plain goodness?
Those are the REAL accomplishments,
the ONLY important ones. THAT'S life.

...unforgettable

It's been awhile since I heard a fingernail
scrape across a blackboard — but I
haven't forgotten the sound! It's funny
how some sounds — and sights — are
unforgettable. Some people are too. Some
are a sight! Some are a scream! Some are
just wonderful to be with because you
KNOW they care about you. They listen.
They compliment. They sympathize. They
suggest gently. They really try to
understand. Make YOURSELF one of
those unforgettable people. That's life!

THAT'S LIFE!

...in the workaday whirl

...in one paragraph or less

Filling out a job application can be almost as much fun as going to the dentist! In a few short paragraphs you're supposed to tell EVERYTHING you've done with your life — and tell how WELL you've done it! But even when you're NOT looking for a new job, it's a good idea to stop, look, and listen to yourself. No matter how perfect you are, there MIGHT be room for improvement. That's life!

...playing the game

Play ball! Be a team player...hit a homer...run, run...slide, slide. Wait a minute — we're not talking baseball here. We're talking business! Today everybody's expected to be a winner and know how to "play the game." So if you're stressed by success — or the lack of it — take a seventh-inning stretch. Think about whether you really believe in the rules your team plays by. Do they play fair? Do you? That's life.

...mixed signals

Are you suffering from a case of mistaken identity?

You're not sure you are what other people think you are...you're not sure you are who YOU think you are...you're not sure WHO you are?

In today's world there are so many conflicting signals: Be an achiever, don't be so uptight; life is serious, smile; beat that deadline, relax.

Don't let the world decide YOUR identity. YOU call the signals! Be true to your own values, faith, and commitments. That's life.

...all steamed up

It's not easy to keep your cool when you're hot under the collar!

Wouldn't you just love to throw a tantrum sometime and act like a mean "widdle" kid — stomp your feet, scream and shout, and turn red in the face?

Tantrums are a sign of frustration. So the next time you get full-to-the-top with frustration, stick a Popsicle in your mouth and a cool thought in your head and think it through, talk it out. That's life.

...getting by and ahead

When you get your first job, you hope you'll make enough money to just get by...but soon "getting" is not enough...you have to get ahead...and the more ahead you get, the more ahead you want to get...but you never get enough. So don't let life get away while you're trying to get more — just be glad you've got enough. That's life!

...this is funny?

It's no laughing matter! I forgot to set the alarm and overslept. Hurrying, I spilled the coffee, tore my stockings, stepped on the dog's tail, and backed my car over a garbage can. After that, the day got even worse. It was no laughing matter. Or was it? When things go wrong, you can laugh or cry — but it's a lot more fun to laugh. That's life.

...subtract cash

Do you have a dream, a goal, a wish? Well, what are you doing about it? Just daydreaming or working? One day my boss gave me an important but difficult job. He said, "ANYBODY can do this job with plenty of money, brains, and hard work. Let's see if YOU can do it without the money." I've never forgotten that. Maybe you might remember it too — 'cause that's life!

...wondering, wondering

"Are goldfish afraid of the dark?" "Do dogs dream?" "Why is snow white?" Children are FULL of questions. But adults have questions too. "How can I pay the bills?" "Where can I get a better job?" "Why am I lonely...afraid...insecure?" It takes faith AND hope AND charity to live in today's world — but YOU can do it! Believe in others...believe in yourself. That's life!

...the hurrieder you go

Hurry, hurry, rush, rush. You've only got five minutes to make the meeting, ten minutes before the store closes.

Do you find that the hurrieder you go, the behinder you get? In today's fast-food, fast-lane society, if you're not careful, you might PASS UP more than you CATCH UP with! Take time to SEE the opportunities, the blessings, the miracles in your world, just waiting for you to NOTICE and enjoy. That's life!

...a good job description

What's the most important job you'll ever have?

Well, here's a job description. You'll need to deal fairly with others that you meet each day. You should be willing to consider new ideas, take advantage of new opportunities, make new friends, and WELCOME each new morning. You should not kill, steal, lie, or cheat.

And just what IS this important job? Why, that's LIFE. That's life!

THAT'S LIFE!

...around the house

...out of gas

Today I ran out of gas. And I wasn't even in my car!

I was in the kitchen, going over my chore list. The longer I looked at it, the longer it looked. My forward gear went into reverse, my motor stalled, and my turn signal wouldn't. When you have a day like that, there's only one thing to do: Say a little prayer, then reach out and touch someone — and don't let go until that someone mops your floor, cuts your grass, or fixes you a nice hot cup of tea!
That's life.

...holding on

Have you ever held a grudge? How did it feel? Soft and warm and wonderful or cold and hard and lonely?

There are so many happy, hopeful things in life to hold on to — a baby's finger, an honest compliment, a pleasant memory, a smile, a song, a possibility.

Let go of those old, cold grudges and latch on to the warm feeling that can come only from a generous, forgiving heart. That's life.

...on the gravy train

Boy, do I HATE washing dishes! Every day — gooey gravy, yucky egg yolk, unidentified dried-on objects! I guess it's good for me though. It reminds me that each day is like a clean dish — bright and shiny...until SOMEONE dirties it up. Even then, work and love can make it clean again — so bright and shiny you can SEE yourself in it! That's life!

...time warps

Why does life always happen one day too late? You find your dream house the day AFTER it was sold. You come across a half-price coupon the day AFTER it expired. But sometimes we LET life pass by. We put off family outings and adventures, saying, "Later...next week...some day." Too soon the children are grown...then gone. SOME day has become too late. Don't bank on tomorrows. Cash in on todays! That's life.

...blame and shame

All those years while the kids are growing up, every time something gets spilled, broken, or lost, you KNOW the ones to blame! The kids did it! But what happens when they grow up? Oh, oh — the finger of blame may start pointing in YOUR direction! So don't be so quick to blame and shame — either others OR yourself. Forgive and let live. That's life!

...a dandy way to grow

Have you ever observed the lifestyle of a dandelion? Early in the morning you go out and its bright cheery face is smiling in the sunshine. So you pull it up. The next day you look out — and the bright cheery face is back. You pull it up again. Two hours later another bright cheery face! You just can't discourage a dandelion! So when YOU get pulled up, stepped on, and treated like a weed, bounce back like the dandy-lion...cause that's life!

...phew!

I smell something! The word *smell* might make you think of passing a skunk on the highway — OR it can be a magic carpet to transport you to a happy time or place as you remember the smell of cookies baking in Grandma's kitchen, the romance of a corsage, the freshness of newly cut grass, or the sweetness of a just-bathed baby. Forget the skunks in your past. Remember the roses. Take time to smell the flowers. That's life.

...wondering about nature's wonders

Isn't mother nature wonderful? She fills the trees with lovely leaves — then WE have to rake them up! She makes our lawns gloriously green with grass — then WE have to mow it! She decorates the skies with thunder and lightning and WE get all wet! But who's complaining! Other planets don't have daffodils and hummingbirds, summer breezes and dazzling sunsets, ripe tomatoes and watermelon. Mmmmm...that's life!

THAT'S LIFE!

...around the town

...wise advice

Play it smart! Know which side your toast
is buttered on. Look before you lurch.
Today we get advice about education,
career, investments, and how to be on the
winning side of everything — except in
the game of life. Years ago someone told
me how to play that game wisely.

It may sound trite but, actually, it's got a
lot of bite. He said, "It's good to be smart.
It's smarter to be good." That's life.

...it isn't raining rain, you see

The words from an old song tell us to "let a smile be your umbrella." Try that — and you'll get all wet! But you know — it's really a great idea. Today's hurried, worried people NEED encouragement, friendship — and a shower! So the next time you see a warm, soft, spring rain — go get wet! Take a walk WITHOUT an umbrella. Lift up your face and feel the raindrops on your eyelashes. And smile. That's life.

...on the grow

They SAY you should always grow and learn. So I read books, study, and listen — but all those facts just won't stick in my brain the way I WANT them to. THEN I eat one chocolate éclair and every calorie sticks to my middle the way I DON'T want it to! I keep growing — but in the WRONG direction. Well, I guess the main thing is to keep WANTING to grow right and keep on trying. That's life.

...color it sunnier

Did you hear about the little girl who went to a fancy restaurant for the first time and heard her grandma order salad with blue cheese dressing? When the waitress asked the little girl what kind of salad dressing SHE would like, the little girl said, "What OTHER colors do you have?" The next time you have a BLUE day, pick a happier color — royal purple, hopeful heliotrope, funny fuchsia. Color your day brighter. That's life.

...a fortunate fortune

Don't you just love Chinese food — all those crispy noodles and rice and mystery ingredients? And THEN the fortune cookie! The other day my fortune cookie read: "The way to love anything is to realize it might be lost." I've been thinking about that a lot lately. Maybe you might like to think about it too. The way to love anything is to REALIZE it might be lost. That's life.

...hurry up and wait

I've been praying for patience...and I want it RIGHT NOW! I mean, what's taking so long? Why do I have to keep waiting for this? Why can't I get what I asked for faster? Is that too much to expect — just a little patience? In today's hurry-scurry world, we expect to get prayers answered as fast as we can get a cup of instant coffee. But sometimes it takes a "lit-tul" longer. Be patient. That's life.

...life is for the birds!

I watched today as a redbird
splish-splashed in the birdbath, then
soared into the sky, heading for new
horizons. I wanted to fly away
too...leaving behind the day's work and
worry, budget and bother. But as I thought
about the redbird flying into winds and
rain, searching for shelter or a few
crumbs, I knew I didn't really WANT to
fly away from the blessings in my own
backyard. Winging it might be fun for
a while — but not as exciting as the
challenge of feathering the nest for my
crazy but cozy family. That's life!

...changing patterns

Have you ever looked inside a child's kaleidoscope?

It's hypnotic to watch all those bright and beautiful colors and patterns — shifting, swirling, changing — always changing. It's fascinating and fun to see how many different designs the same few bits of colored glass can make.

Wouldn't it be great if we would view the changes in our daily world that way too — not as threats but as fascinating and fun-filled occasions? That's life!

THAT'S LIFE!

...with holiday seasonings

...my true love

On the first Valentine Day, my true love gave to me a tiny golden locket...on the second Valentine Day, a dozen roses...and on the third, a fancy book of love poems. Now he gives to me two turtles for the aquarium, three golden French fries, and a potted pear tree to plant out front — as soon as the ground thaws. Well, poems and posies are nice, but everyday loyalty and love are real. That's life.

...aah, springtime

In April somebody always starts singing,
"It isn't raining rain, you know...it's
raining violets." Oh, yeah...where I live,
it's raining rain. And that means muddy
yards, droopy hairdos, and dampened
spirits. But hey! Now I can blame my
messy kitchen floor, weird hairdo, and bad
mood on the weather! Maybe every cloud
DOES have a silver lining. That's life.

...put a lid on summer

Quick! Grab an old Mason jar, grab a top
— and maybe you can bottle summer!
Maybe you can save the picnics and ball
games, Fourth of July fireworks,
swimming and sunning, and roses in
bloom. No, guess not. Just like a baby
grows too soon into a toddler, then a teen,
then a grownup — summer can't be
saved. Only savored. So savor TODAY.
Make the most of every minute.
That's life.

...labors of love

Whoever thought of this bright idea of Labor Day? Don't they know EVERY day is labor day and woman's work is never done, from early morning till long AFTER setting sun? Do they really think it's a "labor of love" to have giggly kids waiting for you to dish out "spaghetti helper" or sing lullabies or bandage a skinned knee and kiss it to make it well? If they think that — they're absolutely right! That's life.

...let us join together

Aah, harvesttime...Indian summer
days...brisk evenings...the time of year
when families gather together all across
the land to share that wonderful
all-American custom — watching football
on TV! Oh, well, whether it's turkey or
touchdowns, family traditions are terrific
because they build togetherness. Give
thanks on Thanksgiving Day — and all
year through — for family hellos and hugs
and just being together. That's life!

...just checking

Making your Christmas list and checking it twice? Gonna buy gifts both naughty and nice? Well, how about checking once more. Are there some persons on your list who might not GET a gift if you didn't give them one — the poor, the homeless, the lonely? Sadly, some of the Christmas "leftovers" are people. Share your joy with someone less fortunate. That's Christmas. That's life.

...less is more?

Did you ever get EVERYTHING you wanted for Christmas? Piles of packages, gobs of goodies, tons of treasures? Well, if you didn't, be GLAD. Remember, your basement is full, your closets are full, your attic is full — so if you GOT all that stuff, where would you put it? This year, want less, appreciate more. That's Christmas. That's life.